© 2025 Mollie Nelson
All rights reserved.
No part of this publication may be reproduced, distributed, or transmitted in any form or by any means without the prior written permission of the author.

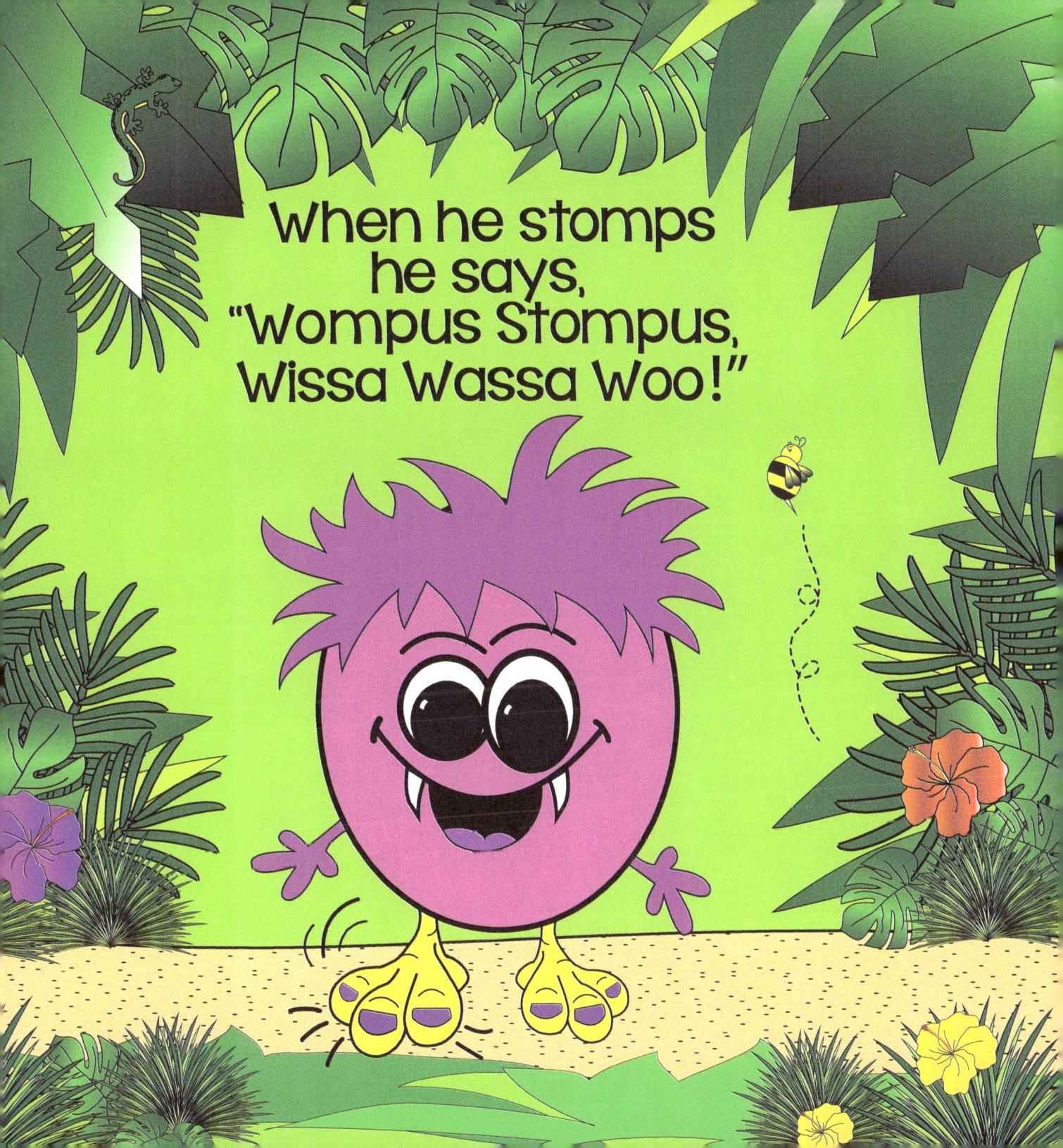

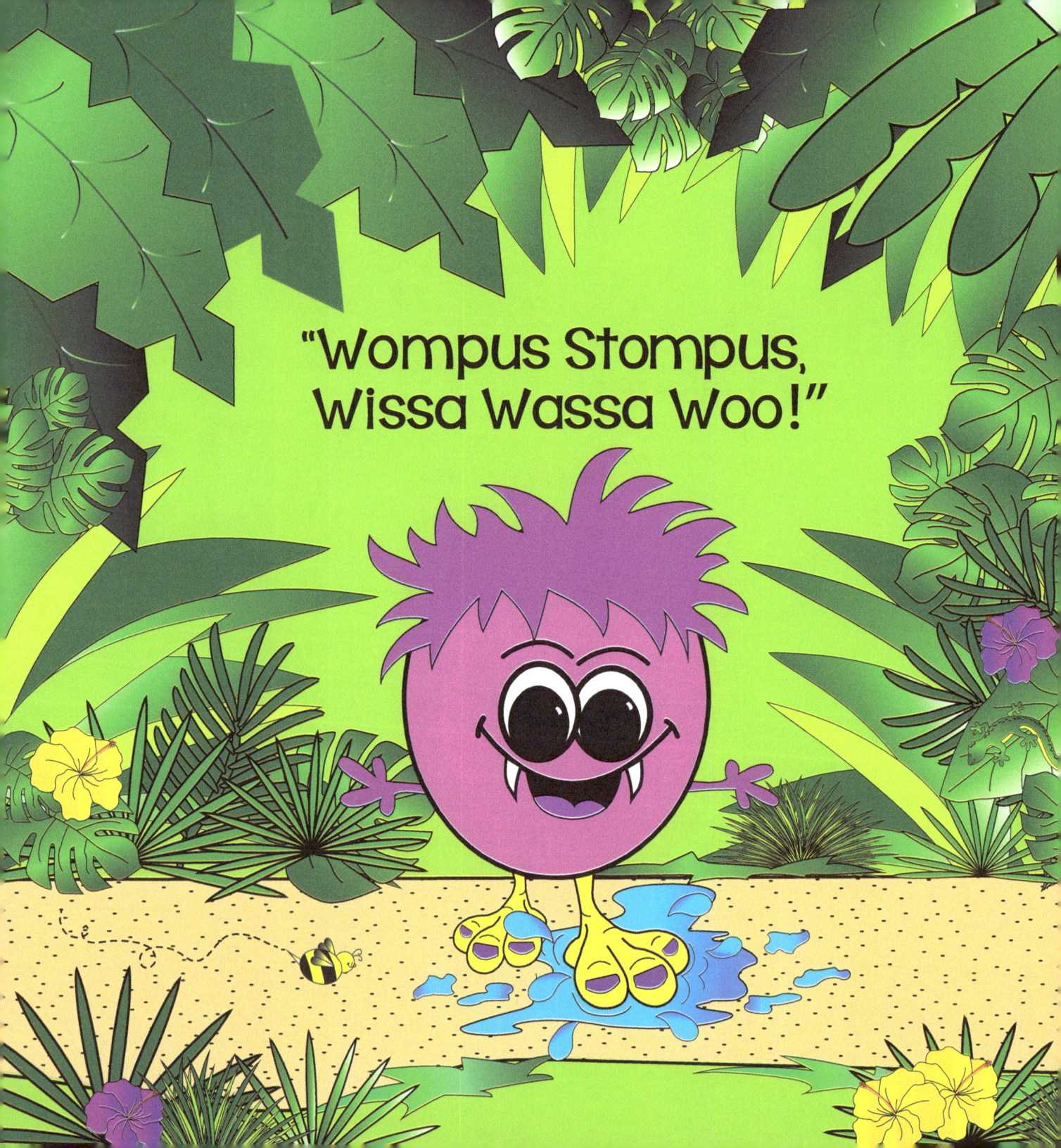

The End

www.ingramcontent.com/pod-product-compliance
Lightning Source LLC
Chambersburg PA
CBHW061350010526
44107CB00011B/892